Exploring a theme: Leaders and Fol...

CW00734724

Contents

For the teacher

This is the first in a new series aimed at helping primary teachers teach RE. Each publication will bring together the practical suggestions of a number of different writers with experience in teaching RE. Our aim is to provide you, the classroom teacher, with some ways of getting pupils thinking and doing in RE. Some you may be able to use as they stand – others you may want to adapt to your own situation. At least they should get you thinking!

In this first issue the focus is on helping children think about who or what inspires and influences them, the significance of key religious figures for religious believers today, and what being a follower means in their lives.

The activities are organised around three main age groups: the Reception class (or Foundation Stage 2); 5–7 year-olds (KS1 in England); and 7–11 year-olds (KS2).

Joyce Mackley (Editor)

The activities in this publication aim to enable pupils to

- describe people and stories that influence the beliefs and values of some religious believers (AT1)

- identify the importance, for some people, of belonging to a religion and recognise the difference this makes to their lives (AT1)

- recognise that religious teachings make a difference to individuals, families and communities (AT2)

- reflect on the sources of inspiration in their own and others lives (AT2)

RE Today weblink:

This series introduces a new service for subscribers. The RE Today website will provide some free additional resources and classroom ready materials. Look out for the 'Retoday on the web' logo at the end of selected articles.

The password for access can be found in each term's REtoday magazine.

Who is special? I am special, Jesus is a special teacher

For the teacher

The following activities are designed to introduce 4–5-year-olds to:

- people who are special to us, whom we admire and why

- two key stories from the New Testament which introduce children to the words and actions of Jesus and his friends, showing how Jesus sets a good example for people to follow today.

Links to Early Learning goals

These RE activities link to the following goals:

- **Personal, social and emotional development:** Children reflect on and talk about a range of thoughts, feelings and spoken words – their own, other people's and those of characters in stories

- **Communication, language and literacy:** Children will also encounter a secular story and two key stories from the Christian tradition, reflecting on their meaning and message and on the words, actions and motivations of the characters.

- **Knowledge and understanding of the world:** Children will think about ways in which people set a good example to follow when they help others and show that they care. They will reflect on: What makes someone special? What makes me special? Why do Christians think Jesus was special?

- **Creative development:** the activities suggested here aim to engage children's imaginations as they express their learning visually and verbally, through talking, writing words and drawing pictures.

Activity

I am special; I have a special friend

- Read a story with pupils about being special, or someone who is special e.g. *Ruby* by Maggie Glen (Red Fox, ISBN: 0099865505) Ruby feels different from other teddy bears – sort of special. So when she finds out that the 'S' stamped on her paw really means 'second' she sets out to show that 'S' bears are far from second best. Or *You are Very Special* by Su Box (Lion, ISBN: 0 7459 3348 3): a book about someone very special – you! Young children learn the value of themselves and others, and consider what makes a person special.

- Ask pupils to picture in their mind's eye someone who: helps them; cheers them up when they are sad and makes them feel happy; takes care of them

- Talk about this, drawing some comparisons between these real-life people and the characters in the story. Questions could focus on: What do you like about this person? Why is this person special? Do you want to be like this person when you grow up?

- Provide children with templates of a speech bubble, thought bubble and feelings bubble as shown on page 3. Use these as a visual stimulus to encourage the children to talk about what they think and how they feel about their special person, and what they would like to say to them. The same can be done for the children's special people: What do they say? What do we imagine they think and feel? Provide key words on cards for children to choose to put in each template e.g:

Happy	Angry	My friend!	You make me smile!
Loved	Hello	I love you!	Warm inside
Sorry	Kind	You're special	Safe
Caring	Thank you!	Fun	Excited

For the teacher

The next two pages help children to explore stories from the Bible about how Jesus sets a good example and how people might follow it:

Jesus is special: Jesus welcomes the children

Faith story

Jesus was tired after a busy day with the crowds, teaching wise things and healing the sick. But people wanted their children to meet Jesus – they wanted Jesus to pray for their children and to give them a hug, and the children kept running up to him. Jesus' friends thought he needed a rest, and they told the children to go away and to leave him alone. Jesus saw this and told his friends off – he was happy to see the children and did not want them to be turned away. He welcomed them and said, 'The kingdom of God belongs to them!' He thought the children were important and special in God's eyes, and that everyone should try to be like a little child.

(Based on Luke 18:15-17)

Activity

- Read or tell the story to the children

- Points to explore and talk about with the children:

  - The disciples turn the children away but Jesus welcomes them. How does he do this? Who welcomes you? Whom do you welcome?

  - Jesus makes time for the children – who makes time for you? Whom do you make time for?

- Make and cut out some templates of a speech bubble, thought bubble, feelings bubble. Enlarge a picture of Jesus and the children. Pick up a bubble and a character at random e.g. the feelings bubble and the children. Use these as a visual stimulus to talk about how the children in the story might have felt. Repeat, using different templates, e.g. Jesus and the thought bubble: what might Jesus have been thinking? Do this several times until the words, thoughts and feelings of the different characters have all been covered.

- Give each child a piece of paper divided into three parts. In one part they draw Jesus, in another part they draw a special person of their own and in the third part they draw themselves.

- Ask the children to write or copy some words next to each picture describing why each person is a special person.

Jesus is special: Jesus helps people

Faith story

One day Jesus was very busy talking to a big crowd of people. He stood in the middle of a big room, surrounded on all sides by people who were listening to him.

Some people at the back had brought their friend to see Jesus. Their friend was ill and couldn't walk – he was paralysed. They couldn't reach Jesus – there were too many people. This made them feel sad because they knew Jesus could help their friend to get better.

Then they had an idea. The building had a flat roof, so they climbed up, removed a skylight and lowered their friend down, right in front of Jesus!

Jesus was amazed at their faith. He thought they were good friends for the paralysed man to have. He forgave the man for anything he had ever done wrong, and he healed the man, who found he could walk again! The man stood up in front of everyone, happy because Jesus had helped him, and happy because his friends had helped him. The crowd was amazed.

(Based on Luke 5: 17-26)

Activity

- Read or tell the story to the children.

- Points to explore and talk about with the children:

  - Jesus helps the paralysed man: How does he do this? Who helps you? Whom do you help?

  - The man's friends are good friends: How are they good friends? How are you a good friend? What do you do for your friends, and what does a good friend do for you?

- Use templates of a speech bubble, thought bubble and a feelings bubble. Copy and enlarge the drawings of Jesus and the paralysed man. As before, pick up a bubble and a character at random e.g. the feelings bubble and the man: use these as a visual stimulus to talk about how the man in the story might have felt. Repeat, using different templates e.g. Jesus and the speech bubble: what might Jesus have said? Do this several times until the words, thoughts and feelings of the different characters have all been covered.

- Ask the children to draw a picture of their favourite part of the story, and to add speech, thought and feelings bubbles. Talk about what the people in the picture might be saying, thinking and feeling at that point. Someone could scribe these for the pupil.

- Ask children to draw a picture called 'the good friend' and to add speech, thought and feelings bubbles to this. What does a good friend say, think and feel?

- These pictures could be done on acetate (e.g. OHTs) with pens or paint designed for this purpose, then displayed as stained glass windows on the classroom windows, like those in churches which show scenes from Jesus' life.

What makes a good leader? Following Jesus the leader

For the teacher

- These lesson suggestions focus on exploring Jesus the leader with 5–7-year-olds.

- The focus question is 'What makes a good leader?'

- Children are asked to consider this in the context of the Jesus story, beginning with the call of the first disciples and then hearing about how Jesus changed people's lives, firstly in his own time (Zacchaeus, the tax collector) and today (composer Roger Jones).

- The material is offered to children through story and guided imagery, with opportunities for them to relate ideas to their own lives.

- Engaging devices are used to help children enter into learning by means of a story and a picture. In another, a story candle is lit to help children understand that they are listening to a faith story – a story with special meaning for believers.

I can

These activities could be used to meet the requirements of an agreed syllabus based on the non-statutory national framework for RE. The following 'I can' statements indicate what most children should be able to do by age 7.

I can:

- retell the stories of Jesus calling the fishermen and Zacchaeus;

- use the word 'Christian' to identify people who follow Jesus;

- say the word 'salvation' and know it was used by Jesus;

- suggest the meaning of the fish symbol for Christians;

- see how the stories of John, Zacchaeus and Roger are similar;

- understand that ideas about God can be shared through music;

- ask questions about what it means to follow Jesus;

- talk about my own feelings and ideas

Information File

- Fishing was big business in Galilee at the time of Jesus. Four fishermen, Peter, Andrew James and John, were called by Jesus to follow him. The story is recorded in Mark 1:14-20; Matthew 4:18-22 and Luke 5:1-11. The fish outline is a symbol the early Christian church adopted.

- Jesus' encounter with Zacchaeus took place in Jericho much later, when he was on his way from Galilee to Jerusalem in the last weeks of his life. It is recorded in Luke (19:1-10).

See Also

- For information suitable for children on the Christian fish symbol, see: http://www.request.org.uk/infants/symbols

- Downloadable PowerPoint telling the story of Zacchaeus suitable for use in school: www.sermons4kids.com/ zacchaeus-ppt-slides.htm

- Roger Jones and Christian Music Ministries, see the CMM website: www.cmm.org.uk.

Activity

1. The story of John the fisherman

Show children a photograph of dawn on Lake Galilee.

You can find many by using Google Images search.

Talk about the scene, explaining this is the setting for the story they are about to hear. It's a story about Jesus, told by John the fisherman.

Chosen to be
John the fisherman

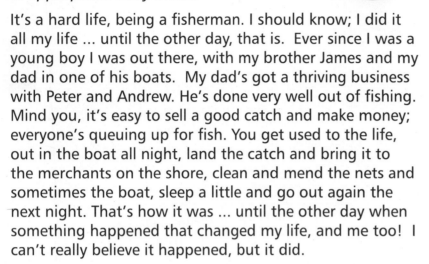

special:
Faith story

*Fade in sounds of water lapping
or appropriate story music.*

It's a hard life, being a fisherman. I should know; I did it all my life ... until the other day, that is. Ever since I was a young boy I was out there, with my brother James and my dad in one of his boats. My dad's got a thriving business with Peter and Andrew. He's done very well out of fishing. Mind you, it's easy to sell a good catch and make money; everyone's queuing up for fish. You get used to the life, out in the boat all night, land the catch and bring it to the merchants on the shore, clean and mend the nets and sometimes the boat, sleep a little and go out again the next night. That's how it was ... until the other day when something happened that changed my life, and me too! I can't really believe it happened, but it did.

We had been out all night and caught very little. The fish just weren't there for us, so we'd come in a bit early and we were washing the nets. A lot of people had gathered on the beach and we wondered why. Then a man came out of the crowd over to us. I recognised him as the Jesus man I'd heard a bit about. He'd been causing some excitement in the next town with what he was saying about God, and lots of people were talking about him ... something about making sick people better ... how could anyone do that?
Well, now Jesus was coming over to us and, as he stepped into Peter's boat, he told Peter to push out into the lake. We were very tired, but somehow it was clear we just had to do as he said. We all helped Peter push the boat out and then I leapt into it.

Jesus stood in the bows of the boat as we bobbed about a bit in the gentle waves. Then, to our surprise, he told us to row further out and throw the net over the side for a big catch. As I told you, it wasn't a catching night, so this seemed a waste of effort, but again we did as he said. Something made us trust him. Then ... wow! When we tried to pull the net in, it was so heavy we had to call another boat out to help us. We heaved and hauled together till the catch was landed and we were puffed out. We've always been good at working together and we don't give up until the job's done, but we've never had to land such a big catch as that one. It felt like a miracle! That was amazing enough but then, as we stood ankle deep in those silver swirls of fishes, Jesus said the words that changed my life: 'Come and follow me and I will make you fishers of people.'

As he spoke, I looked up. His eyes were full of warmth and love. There was something in that look that made me feel he knew all about me; he liked me and saw what I could become. He had chosen me and he made me feel confident. I knew I would do my best for him. I would go to the ends of the earth for him. Afterwards, the others said they felt exactly the same.

We rowed ashore, pulled the boats up and left them on the pebbles, still full of fish. We walked away from our work, from our wages, from our families, from our old lives, ready to put all our energies into following Jesus and helping him; all of us, Peter, Andrew, James and me, just like that, without looking back. I know he's already changed us. And every time I look at Jesus, I remember that look in his eyes and how I felt.... '

(Fade out the water sounds or the story music)

(Story based on Luke 5:1-11)

Follow-up activities

Questions for discussion:

- What questions does that story make you want to ask?
- Why do you think John wanted to follow Jesus?
- What do you think Jesus was like?
- Why do you think Jesus was a good leader? (Draw out some of his characteristics of leadership: charisma, strength, warmth, insight, authoritative air, good judgement and confidence.)
- Who do you know who is a good leader? Who is a leader for you?

For further exploration...

- I wonder what Jesus meant by 'fishers of people'. (Encourage children to explore the metaphor and to think of others.) What do you think it was about the fishermen that made Jesus choose them?

Using think, pair, share strategies:

- Invite children to identify the part of the story that they think is most important and to illustrate it in some way, individually or in groups.
- They could annotate their work with captions or thought bubbles, or freeze-frame the episode.
- Find out more stories about John and the other disciples and their life with Jesus.
- Collect photographs of 'leaders' and talk about their roles.

Talk About

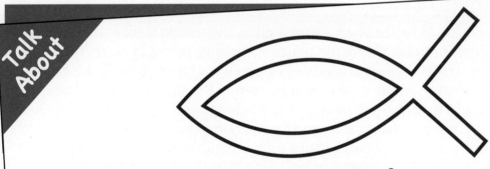

What do you think this looks like...?

Today some followers of Jesus wear a badge like this, or put it on their car. What do you think it means?

Sometimes it looks like this...

Find out what the letters mean.

Why might someone today wear this badge?

2. What made Zacchaeus change?

- Use a photograph of the Sea of Galilee to prompt children's recall of the story of the call of the first disciples. Invite them to think about how the fishermen might have changed because of Jesus.
- Tell children that they are going to hear about another person whose life was changed by meeting Jesus. His name was Zacchaeus. He was a tax collector and everyone hated him because he was a thief and a cheat. Ask them to imagine he can tell them himself about what happened.
- Light a candle. This is an effective way of marking out the special time for listening to a faith story.

Faith story

Chosen to be special:
Zacchaeus the tax collector

'My name's Zacchaeus. I used to be called all sorts of horrid names until a few weeks ago, when my life changed completely. I manage a team of people who collect taxes for the authorities. I used to spend all my time seeing how much money I could make for myself by fiddling the accounts and frightening people to pay me more than they needed to. It was wrong. I know that now, but it took something amazing to make me see just how bad I was.

It was an ordinary day really, just the usual opportunities to make money. There wasn't much else to think about. I didn't have any friends and no one wanted to talk to me if they could help it. Anyway, on that particular day I picked up some rumours that the preacher I'd heard people talking about was coming through town. Jesus, his name was. Well, I was curious. I wondered what it was about him that made him noticed, so I went down to the main street to see him. You wouldn't believe how many people were there! It was as if the whole town had come out to see this Jesus. The crowd wouldn't let me through and as I'm a bit short, I couldn't see over them all. I was jostled a bit as people recognised me and elbowed me out of the way. I got tired of the jeering and name-calling, so I legged it up a sycamore tree. Well, I had a splendid view from up there and no one could see me, which made it even better!

Then the amazing thing happened. As he went past, Jesus stopped on the road and looked up, over the crowd, into my tree. He called out to me ... and he knew my name! He told me to come down and then he said the most startling thing of all: 'Zacchaeus, I'm coming to eat with you today.' With me! No one has wanted to eat with me before — ever! Out of all those people, Jesus chose to come home with me! I couldn't believe it. Then suddenly I saw myself in a different light; I felt different. Jesus wanted to eat with me; I mattered to him. It was a wonderful feeling!

'I will give half of all my belongings to the poor,' I heard myself saying as I tumbled out of the tree, 'and I will pay back anyone I've cheated, four times over.' I stretched out my arms and looked around the crowd. They were as surprised as I was! But Jesus took my arm and said that salvation had come to my house today. And it had, because I haven't looked back. The taxes are collected fairly now and I'm a new man, thanks to Jesus!

(Blow out the story candle)

Follow-up activities

Questions for discussion

- What do you think might have happened to Zacchaeus if Jesus hadn't found him?
- Jesus saved Zacchaeus from being a really horrible person ... so what do you think the word 'salvation' means?
- Who helps you change as you grow up?

Suggested activities

- Hot seat Zacchaeus and explore how it feels to be laughed at;
- Imagine you're a person in the crowd and tell someone else how you felt, or write about your feelings;
- Explore what is the same in the story of the call of the disciples and this story;
- Find and read other stories in the Bible of people whose lives have been changed by Jesus.

3. Meeting Roger, someone who follows Jesus today

Jesus lived a long time ago, but lots of people today follow him and feel he has changed their lives. One of those people is Roger Jones. Roger lives in Birmingham; he used to be a teacher. While he was still teaching, he began to write songs about Jesus for the children in his school to sing. For Roger, Jesus is a wonderful leader who brings people close to God through his teaching and his love. Roger loves Jesus very much. The first song Roger wrote was called 'Jesus rode a donkey into town'. It was about Palm Sunday. Roger knew that children in his school loved his songs so he began writing them for a wider audience. He set up an organisation called 'Christian Music Ministries'. Christian is the word used to describe someone who follows Jesus.

After some years, Roger felt God was calling him to leave his job so that he could spend more time composing music that would bring God-stories to life for lots of people. He wanted other people to know and love Jesus too. Roger and his wife Mary had four children, so giving up his job was a big risk because there would be no regular money to keep the family. But Roger and his friends were convinced that God would provide. They prayed and, amazingly, the money came in, just as they believed it would. Sometimes it felt like a miracle, but their prayers were always answered.

That first song was the start: more than twenty years on, Roger has written 19 musicals and lots of worship songs, which have been performed by choirs all over the world. Many people have listened to his music and been inspired to want to know more about Jesus. Roger believes God has chosen him to help other people love and follow Jesus like he does.

Questions for discussion

- What do you think it is about Jesus that inspires people like Roger?
- What questions would you like to ask Roger, and John and Zacchaeus, if you could?
- Roger believes God has chosen him. How does it feel to be chosen? What would you like to be chosen to do?

Suggested activities

Listen to some of Roger's songs and talk about how they make you feel; invite someone who follows Jesus to talk about her or his faith; work out some questions to ask your visitor, to help you understand what Jesus means to him or her; when you have a list of questions, decide together which are the best ones to ask; draw up a 'job-description' for a leader.

Meeting a rabbi – a leader within the Jewish community

For the teacher

This section is based on an interview with Rabbi Nancy Morris. The activities centre on the role of the rabbi as a leader within the Jewish community and the story of Jonah, which she finds inspirational.

The activities fit well with many agreed syllabus requirements based on the Non-Statutory National Framework for RE (England) themes of Story and Leaders and Teachers.

- Page 11: Children engage with photographs showing the rabbi carrying out some of her duties and reflect on what they see. This encourages the development of thinking skills through reading visual images.

- Page 12: Children match important objects / artefacts to text, and are invited through the use of a simple writing frame to ask the rabbi a question. Look at these together. Ask children to suggest answers that they think she might give.

- Page 13: Children hear the story of Jonah, a favourite story of Rabbi Nancy. The story introduces them to Jewish belief in a God who loves everyone, who wants people to realise when they do wrong things, and to put things right by saying sorry. The activities help children to retell the story, suggest what it means, ask questions and talk about right and wrong.

Expectations

The following 'I can' statements may be useful in setting targets or for an assessment task.

Level 1: *I can....*
- name three things a rabbi does;

- talk about my own special times and places.

Level 2: *I can...*
- recognise some Jewish objects, and say when they are used;

- work out a good question to ask the rabbi about something that puzzles me.

Level 3: *I can*
- make a link between the story of Jonah and Jewish beliefs about saying sorry to God (repentence) ;

- make a link between the teachings about saying sorry in the story of Jonah and things in my own life.

RE Today weblink:

A full version of the interview with Rabbi Nancy and a PowerPoint with colour photographs is available to subscribers on the RE Today website: www.retoday.org.uk

About the Rabbi

Rabbi Nancy Morris lives and works in Glasgow. She is a Reform Jew who finds the ethical and moral teachings of Judaism particularly inspiring. For Nancy, 'one of the most important things to remember, as we live our lives, is to behave properly, act justly and care for the most vulnerable members of society'.

A week in the life of Rabbi Nancy

The word **'rabbi'** means 'teacher', but I do a great many things. I am a leader in my Jewish community and in charge of our special place called a synagogue. I lead prayer services and singing. I visit sick and elderly people. I lead weddings and funerals. Here I am carrying out some of my duties:

I am welcoming a new baby into the community.

What do you notice about the baby and the man?

The people in our Jewish community look to me as a leader and often ask for my advice.

Whom do you go to for help and advice?

This is a young boy's Bar Mitzvah ceremony. It is an important time when boys are allowed to read the Torah scroll for the first time in the synagogue.

How did you feel when you did something for the first time?

Shabbat is a holy day and we have a special service in the synagogue.

You can see me blessing the wine after the service.

Do you have a special day in the week?

Rabbi Nancy says...

Here are some pictures of things that are important in the Jewish religion.

Can you find them in my photographs? Cut out the pictures and the words below.

See if you can match the pictures to the right words.

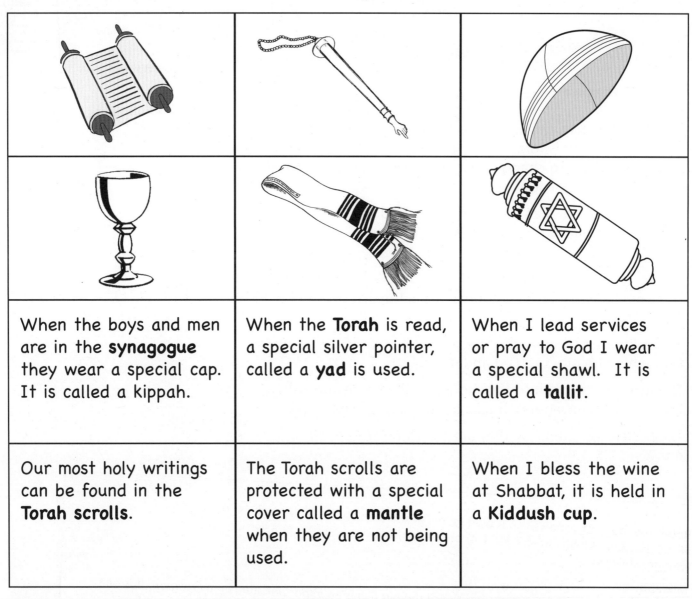

When the boys and men are in the **synagogue** they wear a special cap. It is called a kippah.

When the **Torah** is read, a special silver pointer, called a **yad** is used.

When I lead services or pray to God I wear a special shawl. It is called a **tallit**.

Our most holy writings can be found in the **Torah scrolls**.

The Torah scrolls are protected with a special cover called a **mantle** when they are not being used.

When I bless the wine at Shabbat, it is held in a **Kiddush cup**.

What question would you like to ask Rabbi Nancy?

Dear Rabbi Nancy

....

....

....

....

....

From ....

Jonah – chosen by God: A favourite story of Rabbi Nancy

- One of Rabbi Nancy's favourite stories, and a key story in Judaism, is the story of Jonah.
- The story is told in full on the afternoon of Yom Kippur – the holiest and most solemn day of the Jewish year, a day of fasting and prayers. It is a time when Jewish people say they are sorry – both to God and to those they have hurt. They ask for forgiveness and try to make a new start.
- The key message of the story is that God sees in people things they do not see themselves and that he loves everyone.

Faith story

The story – in brief

- Jonah is told by G-d to go to Nineveh to tell the people there to change their evil ways, otherwise the city will be destroyed.

- Jonah does not want to go, and tries to run away by boarding a boat going to Tarshish.

- On the way to Tarshish, a great storm arises, tossing the ship about. Jonah asks to be thrown overboard as he knows the storm is only because of him. As soon as he is thrown overboard, the storm stops.

- When Jonah is thrown into the sea, he is swallowed by a great fish, where he prays to G-d and is forgiven.

- The fish carries Jonah to the shore, and he heads towards Nineveh. In Nineveh Jonah tells the people G-d's message.

- They listen to Jonah, say they are sorry and start to do what is right.

Activity

Retell the story of Jonah in your own words or use a children's Bible, such as *'The Lion Storyteller Bible'* (ISBN 0-7459-2921-4) or see the RE Today website for a version for younger children.

Talk about:

- Rabbi Nancy says: *'The story of Jonah and the big fish is an important story in my religion. It is one of my favourite stories.'* Why do you think she likes it? What do you think it tells her about God? (God loves everyone and is prepared to forgive those who do bad things if they are really sorry, and try to make things right again [repent])

- Talk together about how God, Jonah and others might be feeling at each of the six points in the story outlined above.

- Talk about a time when someone said sorry to you, or you said sorry to someone else. How did you feel? How did the other person feel? Introduce the children to the word 'repentance'. This is a word religions use when a person 'owns up' to something they have done wrong and asks God and others to forgive them.

Reflective activity: Ask children to choose their favourite moment in the story and write prayers Jonah might have said at this point.

Creative activity: Copy, cut up and give the children the set of six sentences (story in brief) and ask them to sort them into the correct order. Allocate each child one sentence, ask them to make a picture to show that part of the story. Stick or write the sentence they are illustrating on the page somewhere. Put the pictures together to make class books.

Who was Jesus and why do people follow him?
Exploring the 'I am' sayings of Jesus

For the teacher

- Study of the 'I am' sayings of Jesus is a useful way of striking a balance with other RE work on Jesus that emphasises him as a human leader and inspirational figure.

- Pupils are likely to have studied Jesus' parables in earlier years. Parables like the Lost Sheep and the Vineyard are found in the first three Gospels; John's Gospel has parabolic sayings instead, in which Jesus uses symbols for himself. Five 'I am' sayings are explored in these lesson suggestions.

Information File

- The 'I am' sayings in St John's Gospel present Jesus as divine as well as human. This is because 'I am' (Hebrew letters YHWH) is the Jewish name for God (see Exodus 3:14) and in each of these sayings, Jesus comes across as the divine Saviour.

- The seven 'I am' sayings are: bread (John 6:35); light (8:12); door/gate (10:9); shepherd (10:1); resurrection & life (11:25); way, truth & life (14:6); vine (15:1-11).

- Only John's Gospel has Jesus making these 'I am' pronouncements about himself. If John's Gospel was the last of the Gospels to be written, perhaps it reflects more developed Christian beliefs about Jesus as the Christ (i.e. the Saviour).

Activity

Introduce all seven 'I am' sayings in the first lesson and develop pupils' Bible referencing skills. They could match cards with the picture/ the saying/ the Bible reference.

I can...

It is important to be clear about what you want pupils to know, understand and be able to do by the end of the teaching activity. The following 'I can' statements describe outcomes related to the following activities in a pupil-friendly way. These are based on the QCA expectations for most 11-year-olds in RE.

I can....

- use religious words to explain what I think Jesus meant by some of his 'I am' sayings (AT1);

- suggest how the 'I am' claims help Christians to see Jesus as their Saviour and what they feel about him (AT1);

- describe some similarities and differences between different Christian services of Holy Communion (AT1);

- ask some thoughtful questions and suggest answers about the relevance of the 'I am' symbols to my own life and other people's lives (AT2).

'I am the light of the world' (John 8:12)
Key concept: salvation (through guidance and enlightenment)

9-11

Information File

- Light is a symbol of God in the Old Testament part of the Bible e.g. the Psalmist says 'The Lord is my light and my salvation; I will fear no one.' (Psalm 27:1).

- The prophet Isaiah taught that the coming Messiah would take God's light beyond the Jews to the Gentiles: 'I will make you a light to the nations – so that all the world may be saved' (Isaiah 49:6). This idea is taken up in Luke's Gospel (2:32) where the newborn Jesus is declared to be 'A light to reveal your will to the Gentiles and bring glory to your people Israel.'

- In John's Gospel, Jesus is the Light of the World, who leads people to salvation: Jesus said 'I am the light of the world ... Whoever follows me will have the light of life and will never walk in darkness' (John 8:12).

- Jesus also called his followers to be lights in the world: 'your light must shine before people, so that they will see the good things you do and praise your Father in heaven' (Matthew 5:16).

Activity

- Working in pairs, pupils look up Psalm 27:1; Isaiah 49:6; Luke 2:32 and Matthew 5:16. Ask them questions to help draw out the meaning. Look up together John 8:12 and write out the 'I am' saying (beginning with 'Jesus said...') within the shape of a candle, or flame. Write the meaning below it.

- Ask pupils to consider how they can be shining lights, or who is the light of their life and why. A circle-time approach could be used. Pupils could write their ideas in a light bulb or candle shape and create a class mobile.

- Explore further the religious idea of not being in darkness and walking in the light. Make sure pupils understand that Christians believe that Jesus is the source of their inner joy and contentment, even in difficult times. If pupils raise difficult questions that you cannot answer, begin to make a list of them to ask a Christian visitor at the end of this unit.

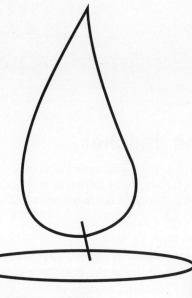

Jesus said....

I think this means...

'I am the bread of life.' 'I am the real vine' (John 6:35; 15:1)

Key concepts: spiritual food; unity with God

Information File

- Chapter 6 of John's Gospel starts with the Feeding of the 5,000. This is the only miracle that is recorded in all four Gospels, and is one of the few miracles in John's Gospel.

- In John's Gospel, miracles are carefully selected as 'signs' to help people understand who Jesus really was – and this is drawn out in the teaching that follows the signs.

- The meaning of this 'I am' saying is that spiritual food is far more important than physical food: 'Do not work for food that goes bad; instead, work for the food that lasts for eternal life' (v.27). Jesus goes on to say that he himself is the spiritual food: 'I am the bread of life ....Those who come to me will never be hungry; those who believe in me will never be thirsty.'

- Christians understand this to refer to the religious symbol/sacrament of bread and wine in their Communion service, where bread represents Christ's body and wine represents his blood, especially since the passage continues: 'Those who eat my flesh and drink my blood have eternal life, and I will raise them to life on the last day' (v. 54) and 'Those who eat my flesh and drink my blood live in me, and I live in them' (v. 56).

- It is appropriate to combine this with the following 'I am' saying about the true vine, because grapes grow from vines and wine is made from grapes. This difficult passage in John 15 verses 1-11 explains the importance of the branches staying on the vine if they are to bear fruit. It teaches Christians the importance of staying with Jesus if they are to be spiritually strong and healthy: 'I am the vine, and you are the branches. Those who remain in me, and I in them, will bear much fruit; for you can do nothing without me' (v.5).

Activity

- In pairs pupils discuss what else we need for life apart from food, water, warmth and shelter. Encourage pupils to explore spiritual things such as love, friendship, protection, guidance.

- Investigate what happens at the service of Holy Communion/Eucharist/Mass in one Christian denomination. A local Christian minister could help you or pupils could view it on video or a website. Allow pupils to taste Communion wafers (unconsecrated). Compare this with what happens in another Christian denomination and identify similarities and differences.

- Interview Christians on the meaning for them of the sacrament of bread and wine. (There may be some pupils who receive Communion.) Do Christians have different interpretations from each other? Can pupils see any links with the spiritual things they explored above?

See Also

www.request.org.
Website about Christianity which includes a PowerPoint on communion.

'I am the resurrection and the life' (John 11: 25)

Key concept: life after death

Information File

- According to John's Gospel, Jesus made this claim in the miracle of the raising of Lazarus from the tomb. He said: 'I am the resurrection and the life. Those who believe in me will live, even though they die; and all those who live and believe in me will never die.'

- Christians believe that Jesus himself was raised to life after death, and that he can give eternal life to his followers. Eternal life is the spiritual life that is experienced this side of the grave and that goes on beyond death.

- This quotation from John's Gospel is read out at Christian funeral services as the coffin is carried into the church or crematorium. It proclaims the Christian belief that this earthly life is not the end and is a comfort to the bereaved.

Activity

- Explain to pupils the Christian belief about life after death. Note down any difficult questions.

- Help pupils to explore their own thoughts about life after death. They could start to share their thoughts in Circle Time, before ordering and developing them in extended writing. Encourage them to say what they believe and why they believe it. Children could look at other children's ideas about death on the website: Listening to children http://www.pcfre.org.uk/db/

NB This is a sensitive subject, but it is important to give pupils the vocabulary to talk about these things and time to think through their ideas with support, when they are not forced to confront this issue through bereavement.

'I am the way, the truth and the life' (John 14:6)

Key concept: finding our way in life

Information File

Christians believe that Jesus is the way to God, because he brings the truth about God, and this leads to eternal life. The first Christians were known as followers of the Way.

Activity

What direction do pupils want their lives to go in? Write up their ideas as signposts (e.g. 'Honesty', 'Generosity', 'Kindness', 'Helpfulness') and make a class display. (AT1)

Activity

Drawing together learning on the 'I am' sayings

- Invite in a Christian, such as a local clergyman/woman, to try to answer all the difficult questions posed by pupils throughout this unit.

- Ask pupils to choose the one 'I am' saying that they think best shows Jesus as divine. They should then work in pairs – then fours – then eights etc – until they have come to a unanimous decision as to which is the best one. They should each write a paragraph explaining it.

Meeting a local Christian minister – a follower and a leader

For the teacher

- Enabling children to meet, listen and respond to visitors from local faith communities is one of the best ways of learning in RE.

- Always plan a specific focus for such a visitor. The focus here is on exploring how a Christian minister is both a follower and a leader.

- The activities on these pages illustrate an approach that teachers can use in their own local area. Key steps:

  1. Identify a local faith community leader.

  2. Interview the faith leader. Ask some good questions about: who they follow and why; what is a favourite story or text and why is it important to them; particular things they do which show how their beliefs affect their everyday life. Try to get some digital photographs to illustrate these, together with a brief comment.

  3. Devise some learning activities around these resources. Aim to challenge pupils to think, reflect, apply ideas and ask thoughtful questions.

See Also

- **RE Quest website:** www.request.org.uk/main/dowhat/day/dayinthelife.htm This website contains video clips, PowerPoints and information relevant to many aspects of this unit.

- **RE Jesus website:** http://rejesus.co.uk The encounters section contains brief interviews with sportsmen who follow Jesus, suitable for older primary pupils.

- **RE Ideas: Christianity** (RE Today services) Contains photocopiable activities for exploring the question 'What makes Jesus an inspiration to Christians?'

I can...

When planning a topic, teachers need to be clear about what they want pupils to be able to do as a result of their learning. The best way of doing this is to work out some simple 'I can...' statements which link to the expectations in the syllabus.

The 'I Can...' statements for the following activities are given here.

By the end of this unit pupils working at level 4 should be able to:

- devise some thoughtful questions and suggest some answers about what makes a leader worth following.

- give some reasons why a person today might choose to follow Jesus and make a link between Jesus and the kind of person they might 'follow'.

- ask some questions and suggest some answers about the work of a Christian pastor.

- make a link between what Jesus said and did, and how Christians today live and what they believe.

Challenging the able

Pupils could use the RE Quest website to find out about the work of another Christian church leader, and make a chart to shows ways in which he or she is similar to and different from John, the minister featured here.

 RE Today weblink: a full version of the interview with colour photographs is available to subscribers on the RE Today website: www.retoday.org.uk

Meeting a Baptist pastor

My name is John Lewis and I'm the pastor of Gorsley Chapel. This is a Baptist church in Herefordshire.

What is a pastor?
A pastor is the person who looks after the people who belong to the church. Jesus talked about being a 'Good Shepherd'. The story of the lost sheep in Luke's Gospel (Ch 15) tells us about what a good shepherd does. I am like that 'shepherd' – only instead of sheep I look after people! Like the shepherd in the story, my job is not only to look after the people in the church, but also to go out and bring others to join the church – just like the shepherd went to find the sheep that was lost.

I do lots of things as a pastor – these pictures show you some of them.

7-11

Lead worship

Preach I call people to follow Jesus.

Lead the church community

Pray, study and learn more about Jesus

Baptise and **marry** people

Visit people in the community

Who do you follow?
'I follow the risen Lord Jesus Christ. For me Jesus is like having a friend who is always with you – a real presence – always there for me'.

How do you follow Jesus?
'For me Jesus is not just an historical person, but here today, present with me. I talk to him in prayer. I try to follow his example. My test is always to ask what did Jesus say, what would he do in this situation. I believe God loves me even though I have done nothing to deserve it. This makes me want to love others. We follow Jesus by praising, listening, and praying in worship, by making him known to others and by doing practical things to help people locally and abroad.'

What makes Jesus a good leader to follow?
'Many leaders want people to do things for them – with Jesus it is the other way around. In his life Jesus always did things for other people – he healed them, he forgave them, he told his disciples "If you want to be great, you must be the servant of all the others" (Mark 10:44). He even washed the disciples' feet to make this clear to them – this was something a servant did in those days.'

John the Pastor's favourite Bible story: Jesus walks on the water

Read the story of Jesus walking on the water in Matthew's Gospel Chapter 14 verses 25-32.

Look carefully at the picture. With a partner, talk about what is happening and what the main characters are thinking and feeling. Fill in the speech and thought bubbles with the things you think the characters are saying or thinking. Then fill in the Explanation boxes as well. Make your answers detailed and clear.

I think Jesus would have said to Peter...

What puzzles me is...

Explanation a:
What did Peter do when he saw Jesus?

Why do you think Peter did this?

I am feeling...

If only I could...

Explanation b:
What did Peter believe about Jesus?

What is your evidence for this?

Explanation a:
What did Jesus think about Peter?

What did Jesus want Peter to have more of?

For you to talk about:
• Why do you think this is the Pastor's favourite Bible story?
• How might it help or inspire him today?

Classroom activities

A good leader: What makes a good leader?

Activity

Ask pupils to imagine they are picking a leader of a new political party or headteacher. Enlarge and copy the following cards. Ask pupils in pairs to sort them to show the qualities they think are most important in a good leader. Give them some blank cards to add their own ideas. Feedback to group.

hard-working	tough	always thinks of others	looks after No 1
organised	trendy	reliable	lazy
big-headed	good listener	visionary knows what they want to do and how to get there	good communicator
makes everyone feel they matter	fair	brainy	strong beliefs
wise	inspirational	brave	

7-11

Whom do you trust?

Activity

Use the line drawing from page 20. Ask pupils to notice what was happening to Peter.

Peter was sinking. He didn't trust Jesus enough. Pupils could:

- Think, pair and share: Do you ever feel like that you are 'sinking' - that everything is getting too much for you? Who would you turn to for help?
- Make a mind map or a poster about the people and things we trust. Write the word trust in the centre and draw/write about your ideas all around it.
- Who did Peter trust? What do you think he means when he says to Jesus 'You really are the Son of God'?

Why do people follow Jesus today?

Activity

Ask pupils to suggest how they might find out the answer to this question.

Things they could do:

- Read the interview with John the Pastor. How might he answer this question?
- Go to the website: www.request.org.uk Go to the 'Do what?' section and look at a video clip of a Christian talking. How might this person answer the question ' Why do you follow Jesus?'
- Work out some good questions to ask a Christian visitor to your school.

Jesus as a good leader

Activity

- Ask pupils to imagine they are the disciple Peter. In groups give them one of the following stories. Printing them on card from a website such as Bible Gateway (www.bible.gospelcom.net/) is helpful.

- Each group could work out one thing the event told Peter about Jesus, giving reasons. Feed back to the group.

  - Simon (who became Peter) first meets Jesus: Luke 5:1-11.

  - Peter sees Jesus with the children: Luke 18:15-16.

  - Peter sees Jesus heal: Luke 8:40-42; 49-56.

  - Peter realises who Jesus is: Luke 9:18-21.

- Peter left everything to follow Jesus. Pupils could use the cards to think about the qualities Peter found in Jesus, adding any of their own ideas. Pupils could then complete the sentence: *I think Peter followed Jesus because...*

How does one Christian family follow Jesus today?

For the teacher

- Whilst all Christians aim to follow the teaching and example of Jesus, there are many different ways of doing this. Recognise this diversity by introducing pupils to a range of Christians who belong to different denominations.

- The activities outlined here focus on a family who belong to a Baptist Church. It is the church where John Lewis is the pastor (see pages 18-21).

- Digital photographs and focused activities are aimed at engaging pupils with the question 'How and why do Christians follow Jesus today?'

- You can follow the process outlined here to develop your own materials. Identify a family who are practising members of a faith community, ask them to take some photographs (or even digital video) to show children how they worship and what they value. Develop some activities that get pupils thinking and doing!

Using ICT in RE

Skilled and imaginative use of ICT can bring 'living' religion into the classroom.

Teachers who use ICT most successfully in RE are those who establish clear RE learning objectives and utilise ICT to develop teaching and learning resources and activities.

I can...

These activities can be used to meet the requirements of an agreed syllabus based on the Non-statutory Framework for RE. The following 'I can...' statements indicate what most pupils should be able to do by 11:

I can....

- use some religious words to describe three ways a Christian family might practise their faith at home and say why they do these things;

- say what difference following Jesus makes to the life of a Christian family, using some religious words;

- describe some things which are the same and different between Baptist Christians and another denomination;

- ask some questions about what Jesus means for Christians and suggest some answers a Christian might give; think about what influences me and talk/write about whom I follow and why;

- express my own ideas about some Christian values.

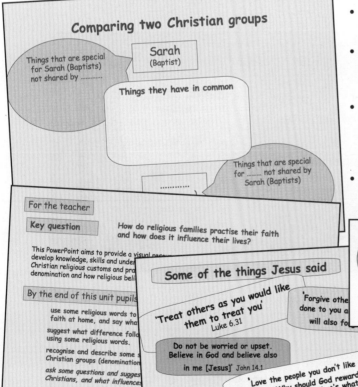

RE Today weblink: PowerPoint 'What's important to Sarah and her family?', combining colour images and activities, is available to subscribers on the RE Today website: www.retoday.org.uk

What's important to Sarah and her family?

This is the story of Sarah and her family. Sarah tells us about some of the things that are important to her and her family

7-11

I try to read my Bible every day. I use some special Bible reading notes for children that help me to learn more about Jesus.

I believe it is important to show people all over the world that Jesus loves them. Every Christmas, as we remember Jesus' birth, we fill a shoebox with toys and gifts to send to children in Eastern Europe.

My name is Sarah and I am 9 years old. I am a Christian and I go to a Baptist Church. This is my family at church on a Sunday – Mum, Dad, my brother, Tim, and my sister, Abi.

Jesus teaches us to look after the sick and lonely. When I know a friend is unwell, I make them a special card to cheer them up.

In the Bible it tells us to give money to the poor. Mum and Dad encourage me to put some of my pocket money into a charity collection box.

Before we eat our tea, we join hands to say a prayer of thanks to God for everything he gives us.

Abi, Tim and I love to praise God by singing action songs together. Sometimes we even do songs in sign language!

For the teacher: some suggestions for using these pictures with pupils

- Photocopy the photographs and statements. Cut up to make two separate packs.

- Give out photo packs to pupils in pairs – ask them to be detectives – look carefully at the 'evidence' in the pictures, speculate about what the family likes doing and what seems to be important to them. Pairs share their ideas. Whole class feedback.

- What does Sarah have to say? Give out the text cards. Ask pupils to match the text to the cards. What does this new evidence tell them about what and who is important to Sarah?

- Ask each pair to work out 2-3 questions they would like to ask Sarah and her family – as a class ask children to suggest some ways they think she might answer these questions.

How one Christian family follows Jesus today:
Some activities to get pupils thinking and doing

What does Sarah read in her Bible?

Pupil Activity

The Gospels tell Sarah about the life and teachings of Jesus.

With a partner, choose one of the following things Jesus said, write it in the centre of a large piece of paper and jot down some ideas about how remembering this advice might help Sarah in her life. Be ready to explain your ideas to the class, giving reasons.

'Treat others as you would like them to treat you': Luke 6:31.

'Forgive others the wrongs they have done to you and your Father in heaven will also forgive you': Matthew 6:14.

'Do not be worried or upset. Believe in God and believe also in me [Jesus]' : John 14:1.

'Love the people you don't like and pray for people who upset you. Why should God reward you if you only love people who love you? That's what everyone else does': Luke 5:43 & 6:32.

'..you [are so important to God]… even the hairs of your head have been counted. Do not be afraid': Matthew 10:30.

Choose one of these teachings of Jesus. How might the world be a better place if everyone tried to live by this? Write or draw and label your ideas.

How and why do Sarah and her family pray, praise and give?

Pupil Activity

Sarah and her family talk to God in their prayers every day. Look at the picture of the family praying around the table.

- What do you think Sarah's mum might be saying in this prayer?

- What are you thankful for? Make a poster to show your ideas.

Sarah says they like to praise God. Talk about what this means.

- Write and draw your ideas around the word PRAISE.

- What does it mean if someone 'praises you'? Do you 'praise' anyone?

Sarah says 'Jesus teaches us to look after the sick and lonely, and to give money to help poor people'

- Write down some ways in which Sarah and her family care for others.

- Make a display to show how Christians in your local area follow the teaching of Jesus about caring for others.

Do all Christians follow Jesus in the same ways?

Activity

Find out if anyone in your school community belongs to another Christian church (there are many different types of churches other than Baptist).

Work out some good questions to ask them about how they follow Jesus at home, at church and in their everyday lives.

Next: You could

- Invite the person to your lesson to answer your questions

Or

- Email your questions to them.

Use the replies to work out how Sarah and her family are are similar to, and different from, the Christian from your own school community.

Who was Muhammad ﷺ and how is he an example to Muslims today?

For the teacher

- The stories on page 27 and 28 can be read to pupils with discussion prompted by the teacher based around the questions at the bottom of each page.

- Alternatively divide the class into two and then into smaller groups of three (make sure at least one in each is a competent reader). Give the groups in one half one story and those in another the other. Give pupils time to work through the text and the questions to explore the meaning of the stories. After this, team each group with another from the other half of the class. Each group tells their story simply (e.g. *'Our story was about a man/woman who ..., the Prophet said/did ..., It means that ...,'*). Groups then share their thinking on the questions they have considered.

The questions for both stories follow a similar process:

1. Pupils will think of a number of titles but, for the first, something like 'Give up telling lies – always tell the truth' and, for the second, 'Showing kindness and forgiveness' would be acceptable. Working out a title for the story helps them consider and express what the key message of that story is.

2. As an alternative to discussion, set up a role-play activity. It is important to remember that the 'character' of the Prophet should not be portrayed. He should *not* be physically present.

3. Encourage pupils to apply the main point of the story to the lives of Muslims today by asking: *'How do you think this story might help Muslims follow the example of the Prophet in their lives today?'*. Develop ideas further for more able pupils by using the stimulus on page 31. This is an extract from the final sermon of the Prophet and what the Imam said about the Prophet as an example to him.

4. Give pupils the opportunity, whether Muslim or not, to consider something of the implications of such an example for their own lives.

I can...

Level 2

- retell the story and suggest what it might say to a Muslim about how they should behave;

- know that Muhammad (pbuh) is an important person and a good example for Muslims to follow;

- *ask questions about whether what the man (or woman) did was right or wrong and say why;*

- *talk about what I think is right and wrong.*

Level 3

- make a link between the story and what it says about why the Prophet is important to Muslims;

- *ask questions about why the story is important to Muslims and say what I think about it.*

Information File

- Muhammad ﷺ – the son of Abudullah and Aamenah and the grandson of Abdul-Muttalib. Muslims believe he is a descendent of the Prophet Ismael, the son of the Prophet Abraham (peace be upon them). Born in Makkah in Arabia in 570CE, his prophetic mission began when he received the first divine revelation in 610CE. He died in 630CE.

- ﷺ Peace be upon him (pbuh)– on saying the name of the Prophet Muslims use this phrase as a sign of respect. It means 'peace be upon him'.

- The Qur'an recognises 25 Prophets, all of whom are respected by Muslims. Muhammad (pbuh) is the final and greatest.

- He is seen as an example of faith and devotion to Allah, the one whom Allah chose to receive the revelation of the Qur'an.

- Muslims believe the Qur'an is the lasting miracle of Allah revealed through the Prophet.

1 Following the Prophet's example

One morning a man who had done many bad things went to the Prophet Muhammad ﷺ to ask for advice about how he could live a better life. He said, 'You are the Prophet sent from Allah, you are a good man and I am a man who does very bad things. Please tell me which of the many bad things I do that I should try to give up first?' The Prophet thought for a moment and then replied, 'Give up telling lies – always tell the truth.' The man promised to follow the Prophet's advice and went home.

That night the man was getting ready to go out – he was planning to break into a house to steal, something he did regularly. Before setting out he thought of his promise to the Prophet. 'If tomorrow I'm asked what I did what will I say? If I say I've been out stealing then people will hate me and call me a thief. But I've promised not to tell a lie. What can I do?' He decided not to steal that night or any other night – he gave up stealing.

Next day he decided to get drunk, something he did regularly. As he poured out his first glass of wine he thought to himself, 'What if the Prophet asks me what I did today? I cannot tell a lie'. So he poured the wine away – and gave up getting drunk.

In this way whenever the man thought of doing something bad he remembered his promise to never tell a lie and always tell the truth, and one by one he gave up all the bad things he did – he became a good Muslim and a very good person through following the Prophet's advice.

For you to think about and do:

1. Make up a title that would 'get across' the key point of this story.
2. Imagine that the man hadn't taken the Prophet's advice. What might have happened to him?
3. What does this story tell you about how Muslims should try to live today?
4. What do you think is a good piece of advice to live by?

2 Following the Prophet's example

Faith story

Not everyone liked the message that Muhammad ﷺ preached. Some people were very angry at his message, which encouraged them to stop believing in many idols and believe instead in Allah. Muhammad ﷺ taught that believing in Allah meant being kind and respectful to everyone – young and old, male and female, rich and poor – because he taught that Allah created and cares for all.

Every day, on his way to the mosque to pray, he passed the house of an old woman. This woman disliked Muhammad's ﷺ message and every day she threw her rubbish out just as he passed by – sometimes it hit him and sometimes it missed him, sometimes he had to walk through it. Every day the Prophet took this insult quietly and calmly and didn't let it disturb him as he went to pray.

One day he passed the woman's house and much to his surprise no rubbish was thrown at him. He asked a neighbour about where the woman was and found out that she was in bed, very ill. He asked permission to go to see her. When the woman saw the Prophet enter her room she thought he'd come to take his revenge out on her now that she was ill. Instead the Prophet asked if there was anything he could do to help her. The woman was amazed at the love and kindness that Muhammad ﷺ showed to her, and his example led her to believe in Allah and to begin to live the Muslim way of life.

For you to think about and do:

Activity

1. Make up a title that would 'get across' the key point of this story.

2. Imagine that you are the old woman, now recovered, talking with her neighbours about why she now follows the Prophet's teaching. What do you think she would say?

3. What does this story tell you about how Muslims should try to live today?

4. When and how do you show kindness to others?

Meeting an Imam – a leader and a follower in Islam

For the teacher

Page 30: Use the stimulus sheet on this page to get pupils thinking about what an imam is and does. Find out more using websites such as Islamic Society of Britain: http://www.isb.org.uk/ or a site which answers children's questions about Islam: http://www.islam4schools.com/. Also use video material, conversations with local Muslims or, ideally, visit the mosque.

Page 31: Use the quotations from two different Muslim sources to focus discussion on the importance of the Qur'an and the example of the Prophet. This activity works best in 2s or 3s with the final question as an individual task.

Page 32: Adapts the ideas on page 31 by giving some concrete examples of decisions to be made. This could be used with pupils in need of more support.

I can...

Level 3

- describe some ways in which the imam shows he is following the teachings of the Prophet and the Qur'an;

- ask questions about why Ahmed Dahdouh might have wanted to become an imam;

- talk about what is important to me in my life.

Level 4

- show that I understand why the Prophet is important to Imam Dahdouh;

- describe how important the Qur'an is to Muslims and say why;

- suggest why being an imam is important to Ahmed Dahdouh.

Level 5

- describe how being a Muslim affects all aspects of life for Ahmed Dahdouh and other Muslims;

- explain how the teaching of the Prophet and the Qur'an is used by Muslims to provide answers to life's 'difficult questions';

- explain what and/or who inspires and influences both Ahmed Dahdouh and myself.

Imam Ahmed Dahdouh

- Ahmed Dahdouh is Imam at the Muslim Cultural Centre in London W10.

- He was born and brought up in Morocco. By the age of nine he could recite the whole of the Qur'an by heart.

- He came to England nine years ago and was imam in Brixton before moving to his present position five years ago.

- He is married with three young children.

9-11

The role of the imam

Information File

- An imam is an educated person who is chosen by the congregation because he is regarded as a good Muslim and because of his knowledge of the Qur'an and of Islam.

- 'Imam' means 'in the front' and describes the imam's main function which is to lead 'salah' (the set prayers).

- The imam also often preaches the sermon (the 'khutbah') at the Jumu'ah (Friday prayers); he teaches people of all ages about Islam, particularly children who need to learn to read the Qur'an in the original Arabic; he takes part in religious ceremonies and acts as a counsellor giving people advice.

RE Today weblink:

Colour photographs used in this article are available to subscribers on the RE Today website: www.retoday.org.uk

An imam

An imam is a Muslim religious leader. He has many tasks to do as part of his work for Allah and for the community.

Each Friday he preaches at the midday Jumu'ah prayers.

Salah is led in the mosque by the Imam five times each day.

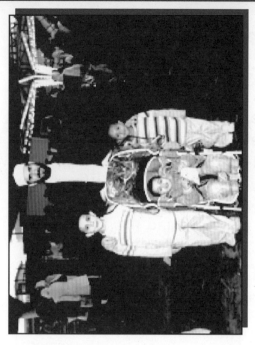

The Imam joins in celebrations with the community. Here he is enjoying the Eid celebrations with his children.

About Imam Ahmed Dahdouh

- He is Imam at the Muslim Cultural Centre in London W10.
- He was born and brought up in Morocco. By the age of nine he could recite the whole of the Qur'an by heart.
- He is married with three young children.

Imam means 'in the front'. His main function is to lead the prayers.

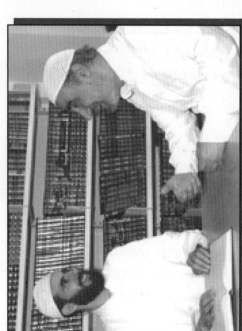

He also has an important role in helping members of the community with problems, and especially in understanding the teachings of the

Examples to follow

Source A

'You have been left Allah's holy book, the Qur'an. If you hold fast to it, and do not let it go, you will not stray from the right path. People, think deeply about my words. I leave behind me two things – the Qur'an and the example of my life. If you follow these you will not fail.'

An extract from the words from the Prophet's farewell sermon

Source B

'The Prophet is important to me because he is Allah's Messenger who brings good news (glad tidings) of Allah at work in all the world. It was through the Prophet that Allah chose to reveal the Qur'an and the Prophet is a good example to look to. He lived an exemplary life serving Allah in the world.'

Imam Ahmed Dahdouh

Activity

To talk about and do

1. The Prophet said he left behind two things for Muslim people to take seriously if they wanted to live a good life. What were they?

2. Which three reasons does the Imam give for Muhammad☪ being important to him?

3. Make a list of some of the things that the Imam does. At the side of each, show how these might be putting the words of the Qur'an or the example of the Prophet into practice. For example: 'The Imam prays 5 times a day – Muhammad said Muslims should do this.'

4. What does the word 'inspiration' mean? In what ways do you think the Prophet or the Qur'an act as an 'inspiration' to Muslims?

5. How might Imam Dahdouh be an inspiration for others in his community?

6. Take the word 'inspiration' and write an acrostic poem to explain what the Imam might find 'inspirational', or write one for yourself showing what or whom you find to be 'an inspiration'.

What would you do if...

A Someone is being bullied in the playground. You don't know the person. Your friend is joining in with the bullying.

B You have forgotten to do your homework and you know you will be in trouble.

C You want some new trainers but your mum can't afford the ones you want. You find a purse with £60 in it just inside the school gates. No one else is around.

- Choose one of these situations.
- Think of two different things you might do. What might be the consequences of each?
- Think up another situation you could be faced with and do the same.
- Present your ideas to the class

What might a Muslim do?

Read the following. What do you think a Muslim might do if faced with one of the situations (a,b,c) above? Be ready to give reasons for your answer.

Two key questions which help Muslims to decide what to do when faced with a decision in life are:

What does the Qur'an teach us?

What would the Prophet do in this situation?

Prophet Muhammad's ﷺ family was not a rich one. He was orphaned and lived first with his grandfather and later with his uncle. He knew sadness in his life. He spent much of his childhood looking after animals and later worked as a merchant trader. He grew up to have excellent manners and because of the honesty in everything he did he earned the nicknames 'al-Saadiq' (the Truthful One) and 'al-Amin' (the Trustworthy One).

'When Allah tells us that the Prophet is the best example for us, it means that whoever we are, whatever our job, we have a role model in him. By thinking about the sort of person he was and how his actions were honest and noble and trying to act in those ways too, we can improve ourselves and live good lives as Allah intends us to do. By taking the Prophet's example into everything we do, we can, God willing, be better people.'

Imam Ahmed Dahdouh